STRAW BALE GARDENING:

No-Dig Gardens Growing Vegetables With Straw Bales

James Paris

Blog: www.planterpost.com

Published By

www.deanburnpublications.com

Copyright © 2014, 2015, James Paris

All rights reserved. Copyright protected. Duplicating, reprinting, or distributing any of the material contained in this work in any form, without the express written consent of the author is prohibited.

While reasonable attempts have been made to assure the accuracy of the information contained within this publication, the author does not assume any responsibility for errors, omissions or contrary interpretation of this information, and any damages incurred by that.

The author does not assume any responsibility or liability whatsoever, for what you choose to do with this information.

***

1st Published September 2014

2nd Print Edition November 2014

3rd Print Edition March 2015

ISBN-10: 1502519569

ISBN-13: 978-1502519566

Other Relevant Titles by James Paris

Raised Bed Gardening 5 Book Bundle

Companion Planting

Growing Berries

Square Foot Gardening

Compost 101

Vegetable Gardening Basics

Small Garden Ideas

James Paris is an **Amazon Best Selling Author**, you can see the full range of books on his Amazon author page here..

http://amazon.com/author/jamesparis

Table of Contents

Contents

Introduction To Straw Bale Gardening..7

   1 - Cheapest Way To Grow: 9

   2 - Exceptionally productive:...12

   3 - Easy Pest Control: 13

   4 – Perfect No-Dig Gardening Solution:..............................14

   Summary:...14

Setting-up Your Straw Bale Garden In 4 Easy Steps................18

   Step 1- Location:..18

   Step 2 - Bale Type – Straw or Hay?.....................................22

   Step 3 - Bale Preparation: 25

   Step 4 - Planting Out The Bale: 30

Planting Tips & Techniques 33

   Plant Support: 38

   The Water Issue: 42

   Alternative Layouts: 44

Some Choice Vegetables To Grow:...47

Top Ten Veggies...50

   Beets: 50

   Bell Peppers:..53

   Cabbage: 56

   Carrots: 58

Cucumber: 62

Green Beans:...66

Leeks:..70

Onions:..75

Potatoes:..80

Tomatoes: 86

From The Author: 91

Introduction To Straw Bale Gardening

There is no doubt about it, gardening can be hard work! That's the bad news. The good news is that it does not have to be *hard* work and there are many different ways to grow excellent vegetables with the minimum of effort.

However I will not lie to you – *minimal effort* is still effort! And like most things in life the more you put in to it, then the greater will be your reward.

This book is all about one of the ***fastest growing*** (pun intended!) gardening methods making the headlines at the moment, and the reasons for this are plentiful as we shall see.

A Brief History:

Growing vegetables in straw of hay is not a new idea. In fact many ancient civilizations including the Aztecs and the Egyptians are recorded as using this concept. The Picts and Celts of early Scotland also grew vegetables in their 'middens' which typically consisted of piles of straw bedding from the animal pens.

After the invention of the baling machine in the 1940's (this produces the small rectangular bales), the opportunity arose for the modern concept of straw bale gardening that we see today.

This technique was used to grow vegetables commercially in the USA in the 1950's. The idea was taught in Europe throughout the 20th century. And more specifically by a Polish professor Tadeusz Pudelski (1926–2012), who published details off, and taught this at Poznan University of Life Sciences in and around 1971.

In effect the idea behind Straw Bale Gardening is not new. What we have now I would call a modern slant on a very old and established idea – and it works!

With that said, I believe the idea behind growing vegetables in straw (or indeed hay) bales has 'come of age' at this time for a number of different and very relevant reasons – not the least of which being environmental considerations.

Straw Bale gardening:

The concept of growing vegetables in straw bales may seem a little strange if you have never come across the idea before, but it has many advantages over traditional row gardening, and indeed several advantages over the popular Square Foot, and Raised Bed gardening techniques.

So why should you consider growing your vegetables in straw bales? Here are just some of the top advantages that straw-bale gardening enjoys..

1 - Cheapest Way To Grow:

One of the biggest expenses involved in setting up a Raised Bed garden or Square Foot garden for instance, is the cost of the growing medium.

This involves creating a suitable soil by mixing compost, peat and vermiculite (depending on your preferences). All of these materials – especially the vermiculite – can be quite expensive.

On top of this you will have the expense required to build the structures whether they be built from timber or concrete block or whatever – it all has to be paid for.

Container gardening also requires a good compost mix, plus the cost of the containers themselves, unless of course you are recycling tires, pots, or broken pails to act as growing containers.

Am I 'dissing' Raised Bed or Square Foot gardening methods? Definitely not – just check out my author page and you will see I have plenty material promoting them!

However it pays to look at all the options available – including straw-bale gardening - if you are to get the best out of your gardening efforts, and indeed choose the technique that best suits your particular circumstances.

You may well argue that 'dirt is cheap' and that growing vegetables in the ground is even cheaper than using a straw bale? The fact is that ground suitable to grow excellent crops does not just 'happen,' unless you are one of the fortunate few to occupy land that is exceptionally productive for whatever reason – usually because it has been well looked after by previous owners!

The vast majority of the time, the soil has to be worked and nurtured if it is to produce good crops. This means the addition of nutrients through either organic means (the best) or through chemical fertilisers (not recommended).

On a side note here…Chemical fertilisers feed the plants, while organic fertilisers feed the soil – which then feeds the plants over a prolonged period. This is the more natural and preferred method for growing healthy vegetables.

Back to cost…The reason that the straw bale gardening method does not require much in the way of compost or soil (more on this later), is that as the bale decomposes it produces its own compost.

This means that over the growing season it is continually feeding your vegetables as it decomposes into mulch. *"Unless a seed falls to the ground and dies…"* Ok, maybe a little out of context – but it nevertheless could be conceived as a form of sacrificial giving on the part of the straw bale!

All in all, the only cost apart from a few handfuls of compost and your seeds or plants is the bales themselves. Which at around $2.00 per bale depending on your local supply, is definitely not expensive compared to the methods just described.

Fertiliser is indeed required to give your bale a boost in the early stages especially. However I will show you how to get a plentiful supply of **free organic fertiliser** in later chapters.

2 - Exceptionally productive:

So why should this method be so productive? There are a few reasons for this.

(a) As mentioned, as the bale itself rots down it produces or creates its own compost or mulching material. This in turn feeds the plants, along with the **free organ**ic fertilisers you have added along the way.

This gives the perfect nutrient-rich environment to produce abundant healthy crops.

(b) Another side-effect of this decomposing action is that the growing bed heats up, giving a welcome spurt of warmth to the young plant roots. **A word of caution** here though – do not plant before the bale has stopped 'cooking.'

This in turn means that you can begin planting earlier, which means a longer growing season and more time to produce fabulous vegetables.

In fact it is quite easy to increase your growing season by at least 2 months, if you embrace some of the techniques included in later chapters of this book.

(c) Growing vegetables this way means that the planting area remains weed-free for most if not all of the growing season.

The end result of this, is that the plants are not competing with weeds for the life-giving nutrients needed to promote healthy growth. Your vegetables are living in the 'perfect' environment and so will 'produce the goods' big time!

3 - Easy Pest Control:

Controlling pests is an on-going task for just about every vegetable gardener. With the SB Garden however this task becomes very simple, as the following passages will demonstrate.

Firstly the new straw bale itself is pretty much a bug-free zone (see later chapters for choosing your bales). This means that you are starting off from a sterile growing area, instead of an area that is perhaps already infested with soil bearing cut-worm larvae or other destructive critters.

These pests tend to come out after dark and cause havoc amongst your young plants especially – not so with the straw bale!

Another happy prospect is the fact that slugs do not like the sharp straw, and will generally give the bale a 'body swerve' and leave your plants alone. This is not always the case, and some slugs may just prove me wrong here - but I have found it to be definite advantage.

In later chapters I will include diagrams and pictures on how to keep flying pests such as the cabbage moth at bay – very simple with a SBG.

4 – Perfect No-Dig Gardening Solution:

Out of the many popular no-dig gardening solutions talked about at the moment – mainly of the Raised Bed genre – Straw Bale gardening could perhaps be reasonably called the 'new kid in town.' However it is most certainly a contender amongst the 'no-dig gardening' techniques being popularised at this time.

Whilst the other contenders for this accolade do in fact need a little light digging with a hand trowel or fork, the fact is that you cannot actually do this with a straw bale – even if you wanted to!

The end result of your probing would be that the integrity of the bale would break down prematurely, and your plants would suffer the consequences.

However…I will conceded that at the end of the growing season you will probably be able to indulge in a bit of digging – when you add the remains of your now mulched-up straw bale to the compost heap!

Summary:

There are many other benefits that can be realised through Straw Bale gardening, most of these can however be effectively shared with the other forms of no-dig gardening such as Raised Bed, Square Foot and Container gardening.

For arguments sake therefore I thought it would be a good idea to make a short-list of these shared benefits in (no particular order), just in case you should be in any doubt as the value of considering alternative vegetable gardening methods.

Check out this list below – which is not conclusive by any means.

1. The SBG is arguably more productive when it comes to crop yield, and the amount of space required to produce amazing crops.

2. Far easier to operate and maintain than a traditional vegetable garden.

3. Weed-free gardening with no need to spend hours hoeing between rows of vegetables to remove weeds. This is mainly due to the fact that you are using a 'clean' growing medium free of weed seeds.

4. Wheelchair friendly gardening, as straw bales can be made accessible from the chair with regard to height and space between the beds for mobility and ease of access.

5. Longer growing seasons are enjoyed by straw bale gardening techniques, as the growing medium is raised from the ground and warms quicker that traditional beds.

6. Pests and bugs are far easier to control as the growing area is already raised up from the ground, and is easier to cover and control pests through the use of nets and companion planting techniques.

7. Back-ache free gardening can be a huge benefit of all Raised Bed systems – of which Straw Bale is also a member.

The simple fact that you are not constantly bending over double to maintain your vegetables, means that back-ache is no longer such a big issue!

8. Bad soil and sloping ground is no longer an issue with these systems, all of which can be easily adapted to suit almost any environment.

9. Cheaper to operate than a Raised Bed system as there is little or no compost needed. The Straw Bale itself produces most of the growing medium required as it decomposes.

10. SB Gardens are a great talking point! The fact that the concept is largely unknown to many people, means that gardeners are intensely interested when you show them your Straw Bale garden :)

The list goes on and on …

NOTES/ TO-DO PAGE

Setting-up Your Straw Bale Garden In 4 Easy Steps

Now that we have looked at the 'why to' it is time to look at the 'how to' part of setting up your Straw Bale garden.

Apart from the obvious question as to what you are going to plant in your veggie garden - there are 4 main steps when it comes to actually going about the business. They are **location**, the **bale type**, **preparation**, and **planting**.

Each of these steps will be looked at in greater detail in the following chapters step by step, to help you avoid 'rookie mistakes' and get the most productivity out of your efforts.

Step 1- Location:

When considering where exactly to put your Straw Bale garden, then the thoughts regarding sunlight, and shelter from adverse elements are very much the same as with any other vegetable garden.

In order to grow well, most vegetables need a minimum of 6-8 hours sunlight. They must have adequate water and nutrients for their needs, and shelter from strong damaging winds – especially in the case of climbers or tall plants such as sweetcorn or tomatoes.

Other considerations would be the *source of* water. You do not want to have to lug pails of water over a long distance, especially in the beginning stages of a Straw Bale garden – as you shall realise in later chapters.

Water for any plant is best gained through a water butt or even nearby stream or pond, if you happen to be so lucky! The reasons for this is that it is generally warmer, so will not shock the plants.

Consider also that mains water is purified or made suitable for human consumption by the addition of many different chemicals such as calcium hydroxide, sodium hydroxide, fluoride, potassium permanganate, chlorine, sodium bicarbonate, algaecide, and clarifiers to name just a few!

These may (or may not) be advantageous for us humans, but plants definitely prosper better with untreated rain water, so this is top choice if it is available to you.

As with all vegetable gardens another consideration may be the accessibility via the kitchen door! The kitchen is after all likely to be the ultimate destination for your fresh vegetables and so if you do not have to travel far to get your fresh carrots for the stew, then all the better.

Maybe not a major consideration, but it's something to think about none the less.

Try not to place you Straw Bale under overhanging branches from trees or bushes – just as you would with any vegetable patch really.

Many trees produce copious amounts of sap that may contaminate your bale as well as your vegetables, as well as drop insects and possibly disease amongst your plants.

If you are using a tree for its shade value in a hot climate, then you must consider the pros and cons of such an arrangement.

It may well work out fine for you if all else is acceptable regarding the plants you are considering versus their particular requirements.

The bale can be placed alongside a wall or fence with no problem, provided it is getting adequate direct sunshine – without getting roasted!

In fact if you are growing climbers such as tomatoes, peas, beans, cucumber etc, then a wall or fence gives you an immediate advantage when arranging for support.

Be aware that once you have set the bale in place, then it is unlikely that you will be able to move it at all, especially after the first few weeks when it is starting to decompose.

That, and the weight of a straw bale when soaked in water, means that wherever it is set-up, that is where it will stay till the growing season is over at least.

The exception to this general rule would be if you had your bale set up on a mobile platform of some kind. Even an old wheelbarrow would enable you to move it around the garden to get the best of the light or other conditions.

Step 2 - Bale Type – Straw or Hay?

Amongst the advocates of 'bale gardening' this question perhaps causes the most controversy or consternation. The fact is that there are benefits as well as advantages to both types of bales and each should be looked at with due consideration.

First of all, especially if you are not familiar with the 'country ways' – what is the difference?

In a nut-shell, straw bales typically come from the harvest of barley, wheat, oats or rye. This is usually used for bedding animals.

Hay bales on the other hand consist of grass that has been grown to produce feed for the animals over the winter. This is harvested, dried, and set into bales for storage. Sometimes it is mixed 'wet' with molasses to enrich the feed and sealed in a large round polythene bag to create silage.

Things to Consider:

Basically what we have to consider when using either of these bale types for our growing plants, is exactly what each of them 'brings to the table' with regard to advantages or disadvantages.

Straw bales have the immediate advantage over hay in that you will not get a crop of weeds with a straw bale, whereas if the hay has been harvested late in the season then it will be full of grass seeds – which will sprout as soon as you begin the watering process!

However on a negative note – straw bales have no immediate nutritional value, whereas **hay bales** consisting of grass have an immediate nutritional value being high in nitrogen, potassium and phosphorus. This is released through the composting process and adds an immediate benefit for the vegetables.

This apparent advantage is however not as good as it seems, for simple watering with nutrients should add all the benefits that the virgin bale lacks.

In my experience **straw bales are not so greedy** when it comes to watering them, whereas **hay bales need constant attention** to prevent them drying out completely.

This could simply be down to the fact that the straw creates good hollow tubes that keep the water longer, where hay is narrower and more densely packed during the baling process. This could mean that a hay bale is more resistant to watering, and holds less water overall.

This however is not an 'absolute' as many things including your own climatic conditions play a part with regard to water retention or indeed consumption.

Bottom Line?

The problem with weeds is perhaps my main objection to using hay bales, after all how am I to know when the farmer baled the hay? If indeed it was after the seeds had formed, then I will spend the growing season stopping a lawn growing amongst my vegetable patch!

Add to this the fact that hay is generally around twice the cost of straw, and a bale of hay weighs much more (yea I'm an **old** skinflint!).

So my own preference is for straw bales, but if you want to try hay then that's just fine – just make sure the grass cutting shears are kept handy (smile).

I will admit however there is another way to keep weeds under control if you have chosen to use a 'seedy' hay bale. Simply wrap the sides and top of the bale with a weed suppressant fabric. Allow a space for you plants to go through on top, as you would normally.

As an addition, I would recommend in this instance to run a perforated hose under the fabric to water the bale evenly during the growing season.

Step 3 - Bale Preparation:

Now comes the real 'hands-on' part of this gardening technique – setting out the straw bale.

Once you have identified your location the bale has to be properly set-up and primed in order to receive your plants. It is not (unfortunately) a simple matter of dumping the bale on the ground and shoving in your vegetables, then sitting back to behold the results!

Ground Surface:

The first thing to consider is the ground itself. If it is covered in weeds or grass, then you should lay down a weed-membrane either fabric or – better in my mind – a couple of layers of cardboard.

The reason this is important is getting back to the previous chapter on controlling weeds. If you just dump the bale down on top of weeds or grass, then the chances are that some of the weeds will grow straight up through the bale over the season.

With regard to fabric or cardboard covering. Both will do the job of suppressing the weeds, however the cardboard has an added bonus in that it will slowly decompose and with the help of worms (who just happen to love cardboard and paper), will eventually be composted and integrated along with the bale itself.

A win-win situation really as you will have excellent material at the end of the growing season to add to your composting bin.

Another option is to turf the area where the bale is to sit down to 3-4 inches, and then sink the bale inside this area. This has the advantage in that depending on your water situation or local climate, the bale can draw water direct from the soil helping to prevent drying out.

Also the fact that the bale is in direct contact with the soil and all the beneficial worms and microbes, means that the composting effect is slightly accelerated overall.

Setting up/Feeding:

When placing the bale itself, it is important that it is arranged cut side up, or on edge. This enables the water to seep right to the inside of the bale and begin the 'cooking' process.

If you inspect the bales you will notice that one of the two cut sides consists of folded straw and the other is clean-cut straw? This clean-cut side is the one that faces upward.

This allows the water and fertilizer to run down to the inside of the bale and remain trapped. It is not a complete disaster if you get this wrong, but the bale will tend to dry out quicker as it will not hold the water as efficiently.

The 2 strings that hold the bale in place should be running along the sides. It is important that you leave these strings in place – for obvious reasons!

This 'cooking' is where the bale begins the process of decomposing and thereby producing heat in the inside of the bale, which in turn breaks down the straw and prepares it for your plants to benefit.

Once you have the bale in place then you must feed and water it to begin the process. Feeding is very important as the straw bale itself is mainly just carbon (hay differs as per the previous chapters), and your vegetables will need a good mixture of nitrogen and potash to develop fully.

This feeding can be achieved in several ways. Either through conventional fertilisers or store-bought organic fertiliser or (my preferred method), home-brewed organic feeds.

The **store bought nitrogen-rich feeds** should be spread over the bale at the beginning and watered in. Thereafter added to the water itself is often best before the bale is soaked.

Organic home-brew is simple to make and apply. Preparation should be done a few days before you are ready for the bale.

Add a few good handfuls of grass, stinging nettles, or borage which has been cut into pieces, to a pail of water.

Weigh it down with a heavy stone or brick, then leave for 7 days to infuse.

The resulting liquid can be diluted at roughly 1 part feed to 10 parts water, then applied to the bale. The remaining liquid can be topped-up over the season with more plant material and water, and applied as necessary.

Compost feed can be produced by taking a few handfuls of compost and adding to water and left to infuse as previously described.

Manure feed is especially rich in nitrogen which your veggies will love, however it is the 'stinky' option! To make this tea place a shovel of manure (horse, sheep, rabbit chicken, or goat is ideal) into a hessian sack and put inside a deep pail of water for 5-7 days.

Squish the sack up and down a bit before removing from the pail (you can add it to the compost heap). The resulting tea should be watered down about 15 parts water to 1 part tea.

Be aware however that using fresh manure does carry an element of risk with regard to E.coli and other harmful bacteria and worm larvae that may be present.

With that in mind do take precautions when handling fresh manure, or alternatively (and safer) use well composted manure that has been composting for at least 1 year.

Also, do not use manure compost on any low-ground vegetables that may come into direct contact with it, such as cucumber or courgettes for instance.

Fish meal, bone meal and seaweed also are great sources of nitrogen, potassium and other nutrients that will benefit your vegetables.

Priming The Bale:

The actual process of priming your bale should be done in the following sequence..

Day 1: Soak the bale completely with water infused with nutrients, or prepare the bale by scattering some store-bough fertiliser over it before soaking.

Day's 2-5: Continue with the soaking and feeding process. Monitor the internal temperature with a thermometer (a compost or meat temperature probe is ideal), and watch for the rise in temperature as the 'cooking' process begins.

Day's 6-14: Water every alternate day, checking to see that the bale does not dry out. As the process of 'cooking out' comes to an end, the bale will cool down to reflect a temperature just a little higher or equivalent to, the ambient external temperature.

This means that the bale is ready to plant. If the reading is still high then wait till it drops before attempting to plant, otherwise it will be too hot for the roots and the plant will likely suffer a premature death!

Step 4 - Planting Out The Bale:

Now that you bale has 'cooked out' and the composting process has begun, you are ready to plant the vegetables of your choice.

There will be more details regarding the individual vegetables and their growing needs in later chapters, for now however we shall look at the steps to be taken in order to get the best out of your bale.

Plants or Seeds?

The first decision is whether you intend to plant young developed plants, or plant direct from seed. Either way is possible for your straw bale garden, but the process differs as per the instructions below.

Planting from seed is possible by covering the flat surface of the bale about 2 inches deep in a good potting compost. This should reach to about 2 inches from the edge of the bale itself.

Once this is done then simply poke a hole with your finger at the spacing's needed for your seeds, and place the seed in the holes.

For small seeds such as onions, then sow sparingly in rows as you would in a conventional garden.

Planting young seedlings is a simple matter of chopping into the bale and digging out a suitable area (usually 4-6 inches deep and 3-4 inches across) and after removing your plant from its pot, placing it in the hole.

Firm around with more good potting compost before watering thoroughly.

Stand back and admire your work!

Feeding: Although the bale should by now be thoroughly infused with nutrients thanks to your feeding efforts, your plants will need further feeding especially when they begin to produce fruits or otherwise mature.

Once per week with your organic tea should be adequate for most vegetables. With a heavy crop of fruiting tomatoes however, I would increase the dosage to twice per week

STRAW BALES MAKE EXCELLENT HERB GARDENS

NOTES/ TO-DO PAGE

Planting Tips & Techniques

There are many ways to take best advantage of your straw bale planting efforts, including plant support, protection from insects, early growth and even the numbers of vegetables you can grow to each bale.

There is virtually no limit to the variety of vegetables that can be grown using this system, the main one being your particular location and what is traditionally able to grow due to climatic considerations.

The chart below lists the approximate times for the vegetables planted to reach the harvest stage, and how many of each plant you can comfortably plant in one bale.

Bear in mind that you are able to grow plants closer than you would in a traditional garden layout, owing to the nutrient value and other considerations peculiar to Raised Bed gardening.

In the following chart, numbers must be regarded as approximate as it very much depends on whether you are planting one row up the centre, or two rows, or even 2 staggered rows – diagrams to follow.

Plants	Approx Days to Harvest	No Per Bale
BROCCOLI	85-110	6
BEETS	50-70	15-20
BEANS (pole)	70-80	8-12
BRUSSELS SPROUTS	85-100	6
CABBAGE	90-100	6
CAULIFLOWER	85-110	6
CARROT	70	25-30
CUCUMBER	55	4-6
EGGPLANT (Aubergine)	110-120	3
GARLIC	90-100	16
LETTUCE	40-80	8-12
LEEK	100-125	35-40
ONIONS	95-110	16
PARSNIPS	95-110	25-30
PEAS	70-80	8-12
PEPPERS	70-80	4
POTATO	80-100	3
STRAWBERRY	60-90	4
SCALLION (Spring Onion)	60-70	16
SQUASH	85-90	3
TOMATOES	70-75	3
ZUCCHINI (courgette)	80	3

Carrots and parsnips especially, need a special mention here as they must be grown from seed – transplanting rarely works with these particular roots. When planting these vegetables, instead of the method described for planting seeds try the following method.

When the bale is ready, run a trowel or something similar down the bale in 2 or 3 rows lengthwise, to a depth of 9-12 inches forcing the straw aside as you go.

Part with your hand to create a trench the full length, then fill this with good potting compost. Sprinkle on your seeds sparingly then water.

As the plants grow to about 2-3 inches, trim between them with a pair of sharp scissors to cause the least disturbance to the roots, leaving a gap of about 3 inches between the plants.

These next diagrams give an idea of the different choices available to you when it comes to planting out your vegetables.

These pictures below are how your bale could look like when viewed from above, and show patterns for planting young plants.

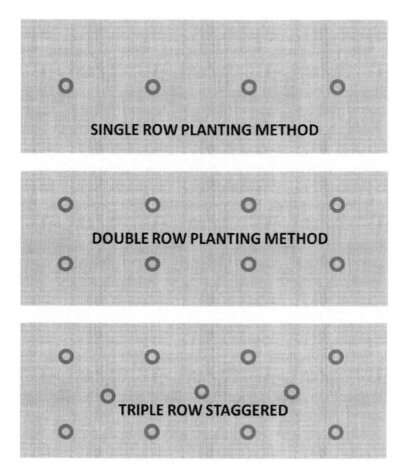

The following diagram shows a bale laid out for planting from seed (other than carrots and parsnips).

Bale Prepared For Seeds

**CENTRE OF BALE COVERED TO DEPTH OF 2 INCHES READY TO RECEIVE SEEDS.
2 INCH PERIMETER LEFT ALL AROUND THE BALE.**

For planting carrots & Parsnips

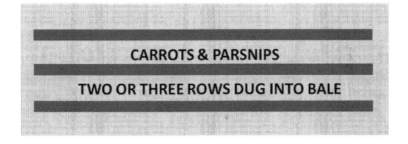

As you can see, there are many ways that you can plant your vegetables, whether by seed or seedling in order to get the most out of your straw bale.

Plant Support:

Of course many varieties of fruits and vegetables need support of some kind, and this is certainly the case with straw bale gardening – especially as the bale itself starts to deteriorate.

Thankfully this is not a difficult task with straw bales, and indeed this technique has some advantages over traditional growing methods.

There are several ways to go about this, from wires strung between posts, to growing up a fence or wall using canes, wires or netting – wire or nylon.

The following diagrams give some ideas as to supporting or protecting your plants incorporating the unique assets of the Straw Bale.

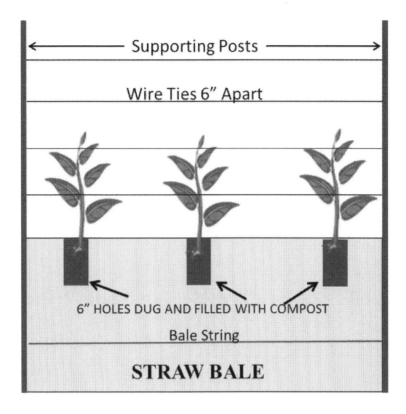

In the picture above you will see one example of a very effective support system. The posts are hammered into the ground at each end of the bale, then connected along the top with a 3 x 1 inch timber strap or similar.

This top brace will keep the frame rigid as you add tension to the wires between the posts, upon which your climbing plants will grow.

Instead of wire strung horizontally between the posts, you can instead use vertical canes, or indeed 4 inch wire sheep-mesh – especially goof for climbing beans or peas.

The advantage the horizontal wire system has though, is that you can easily throw polythene or insect mesh over the wire throughout the growing process; pull it down and tuck it under the strings on the straw bale.

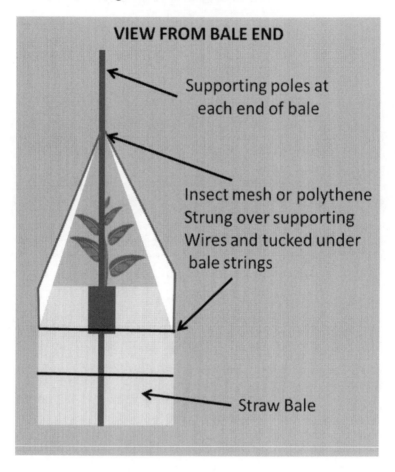

This forms an extremely effective cold-frame for early growth, or an equally effective insect barrier against the dreaded cabbage moth for instance!

With regard to how many bales you can put end-to-end with this method, I find that 2-3 bales is about best. More than this puts a strain on the wire and posts, and generally makes things a bit less manageable.

However if you would like a number of bales to form your SBG then that is no problem. It is a simple matter to form open-ended squares or even longer rows of bales as long as the supporting posts and wires are sufficient to hold everything in place.

The Water Issue:

Water, either the wastage of it or the general supply of it, can be a major issue for some folks for a variety of reasons. And for sure it is a good thing to preserve such a valuable resource whenever we can.

Straw bale gardening can use up a considerable amount of water in some hot dry climates, and so it pays to look at ways to reduce this usage as much as we can while at the same time not jeopardising our planting efforts.

Fortunately there is an easy solution if you feel that the straw bale is using up too much water , or indeed drying out too quickly – **wrap the bale in cling-film!**

Yes, by simply rolling out some kitchen cling-film around the bale 2 or 3 times, you will not only prevent the bale drying out, but also help in the composting action of nature to break down the bale itself – thereby feeding your plants.

This is a method you may often see around farms, as they wrap the round bales in industrial-grade cling-film to create silage for winter animal feed.

Any polythene will do though, as the aim is simply to prevent or at least reduce evaporation. Weed-suppressant fabric wrapped around the bale will also help prevent water loss.

Encasing the bales in timber, brick, corrugated iron sheeting, or anything else you may have handy will all help in this respect.

Finally, be sure that you are making the most of nature's supply. Keep water butts connected to any down-pipes you may have on your house or outbuildings, and store the water for using on your straw bales.

As mentioned in earlier chapters, this water will give you better results with regard to crop yield than treated tap water will.

Alternative Layouts:

Apart from growing vegetables within the straw bale itself, a combination of 'both worlds' means that you can increase your vegetable production.

This is simply achieved by taking a number of bales and forming them into a square with an open centre.

Fill in the centre with good compost – not topsoil as this is likely to compact – and plant out both the bales and the centre with vegetables.

Make sure that you can reach the centre of your construction in order to harvest your produce. This usually means that a reach from the side of your bales should not exceed 3 feet to the centre.

The straw bales themselves act as excellent insulators, often meaning that you can grow vegetables more suited to warmer climates in this centre-growing arrangement.

Use your imagination! There are numerous different ways in which you can place your bales to best effect, and indeed many different ways to protect your plants or create climbing areas – or both!

Bale covered with weld-wire for plants to grow on.

An alternative but similar option is to construct a Raised Bed Garden to the dimensions of the straw bales, and use the bales themselves for infill instead of filling with your expensive soil mix.

For instance if you construct a framework 8 foot long by 18/24 inches high, by 36 inches wide. This would accommodate 4 bales neatly. (Double check your local bales sizes just to be sure before construction!)

The sides of the 'box' do not have to solid in the same way as a traditional Raised Bed, as there is no soil to fall out. This means that you can use less timber, which again reduces overall cost.

You can go even further with a little imagination and construct a good looking framework that would make an excellent piece of patio furniture as well as a good talking point with friends and family.

Need more? If you add a timber base to the frame, then attach some wheels, you can have a mobile Raised Bed SBG!

This can be a fantastic addition, as one of the other benefits includes the ability to wheel it around to follow the sun! I would however only recommend this on a smaller single bale construction.

Some Choice Vegetables To Grow:

Now that you have all the information you need to start your very own Straw Bale gardening project. Here in this next chapter are some vegetables you may well consider growing.

This material is in the main 'borrowed' from my book on vegetable gardening 'Vegetable Gardening Basics' (no use trying to re-invent the wheel!) I hope you enjoy!

Although these instructions are aimed at traditional growing practices, the requirements regarding your straw bale vegetables are pretty much the same, with some minor modifications.

Armed with the information in the previous chapters and with a little imagination, all of these vegetables can be grown very successfully in a Straw Bale garden.

Crops such as potatoes, carrots and parsnips do require some 'special care' when it comes to growing in straw bales. This is mentioned in more detail either in the previous chapter on 'Planting out the bale' or as in the case of potatoes, in the relevant chapter following.

Bear in mind that all these vegetable crops can in effect be grown slightly earlier than indicated for the traditional planting methods. This is due to the fact that the straw bale itself is well insulated against the cold weather, and is not so much subject to ground temperatures.

Also some of the issues mentioned in the following notes involving pests such as the cutworm and other soil-dwelling critters, thankfully are not a problem when growing in straw bales.

The general information regarding plant care, storing, and harvesting tips to follow is useful to know no matter what gardening technique you employ.

NOTES/ TO-DO PAGE

Top Ten Veggies

There are of course many hundreds of different vegetables you can grow yourself, depending on factors such as your location, growing outside or in a hothouse, or indeed what you personally like or prefer to grow.

For the beginner to vegetable gardening however, here are my top ten vegetables to try out and get the general feel for growing your own veggies. Laid out alphabetically rather than in any other order, they are as follows..

Beets:

Introducing Beets:
Beets are a good choice for gardeners in Northern climates as they grow well in the cooler conditions. An excellent

long-season crop as they are even able to survive frosty temperatures. Will prosper well in high phosphorous levels, but high nitrogen may result in excessive leafiness and small bulbs. For this reason it is not a good crop to grow in the same ground that legumes such as peas and beans have just vacated.

Planting:

Seeds can be planted indoors to give an early start, about 1-2 inches apart and ½ inch deep, but wait until soil reaches 50 degrees if sowing outdoors.

If temperature allows, planting can begin late March/April and continue until late in the season. Plantings can be spaced around 20 days apart to allow for Beets throughout the growing season.

A good crop for late – even winter crops in zone 9 or above.

Planting in straw bales can be done either by seed on a bed of compost mix (as described in earlier chapters), or planted as seedlings direct into the prepared bale. As described in earlier chapters.

Plant Care:

Thin out the plants when they reach about 2 inches high by pinching them off at the base, or snip with shears so not to disturb the ground. Leave a gap of around 3-4 inches between plants. Beets are prone to rise out of the ground when in the early stages of growth, making them prone to the predations of slugs and other insects, so it is best to press the young beets carefully back down into the ground again until the root system is properly established.

Harvesting:
Beets are usually ready for harvesting in 50-70 days, though they can be harvested any time after the bulb appears. They can be left longer but will become tougher as they grow, and slightly woody.

A highly nutritious and tasty part of the beetroot plant is the leaves, they are also delicious and make a good addition to salad dishes if picked before they get old and tough.

Beets can be stored for many months as long as you have a dry cool dry place. After lifting the beets, remove any dirt and let the skins dry before storing. Beets can also be pickled, frozen or canned to preserve them.

***

Bell Peppers:

Introduction To Peppers:

Second only to tomatoes as a garden favourite, Peppers come in many shapes, colours and sizes, hot or sweet – and modern-day chefs would be lost without them! A simple plant to grow if you have warm enough conditions (average 70 degrees F.) Bell Peppers are a great addition to your vegetable garden or greenhouse.

Planting:
Peppers will not survive in ground temperatures below 65 degrees F. So if you want to grow them outdoors this is the minimum requirement; in cooler climates it is best to grow in a greenhouse environment.

Seeds should be grown about 3-4 to a pot and the weakest discarded, before transplanting the healthy plants to your outdoor growing area (if you are able to grow them outdoors) after the spring frosts are well clear.

They should be planted about 18 inches apart, in rows about two feet apart. Placing a cardboard collar (try the toilet roll insert when the paper is finished!) around the stem of the plant, sunk about an inch into the soil, will protect against stem cutworms.

They are particularly susceptible to root shock if the ground temperature is below 60 degrees F. This can stunt the growth for several weeks so must be taken into consideration before planting out. Peppers have to be supported with canes or some other support such as nylon garden mesh.

Planting into straw bales is usually best done with young seedlings direct into the bale as described earlier.

Plant Care:
This is a thirsty plant so be sure to water regularly especially if you live an exceptional hot dry climate. Make sure the fruits are properly supported and that the plant is not struggling under the weight.

Care has to be taken when weeding around the base of the plants as this can easily damage the shallow root system. Watch out for Aphids and Flea beetles and blossom-end rot - which occurs when calcium is low – usually because of irregular or insufficient watering practices.

They are particularly prone to root rot if there is standing water around the stem, so good drainage is essential to maintain a healthy plant.

Harvesting:
Unlike some other vegetables that grow tougher as they age on the plant; Peppers grow in sweetness and flavour the longer you allow them to grow, and increase in their vitamin C content.

Remove the peppers by snipping the pepper stem, rather than tearing or breaking it from the plant.

Peppers will store in a fridge for 7-10 days in a plastic bag, or they can be sliced and frozen.

***

Cabbage:

Introducing Cabbage:

Cabbage is a popular vegetable with many varieties, offering opportunities for many different growing conditions and taste preferences. Rich in iron, it likes cool temperatures and so is ideal for cooler Northern climates where it is best planted early spring and fall.

Planting:
For an early start to the season, begin by planting seeds indoors about 8 weeks before the last spring frost. The young plants can then be transplanted into your prepared area about two weeks or so before the last of the spring frosts.

During this time protect the seedlings under a cloche or some garden fleece, particularly in the cold evenings, until they are fully established and the cooler weather has gone.

Plant Care:
Young plants especially have to be protected from the predations of pigeons and rabbits, who will simply decimate your plants in short time if allowed! Garden fleece can be used to good effect in this matter – especially against the pigeons or cabbage butterfly. More robust measures such as rabbit mesh will maybe have to be employed against rabbits however.

Caterpillars from the cabbage butterfly, along with aphids and other insects love a bit of cabbage! Check out the section on Organic Pest Control to see how to discourage them from your cabbage patch.

Harvesting:
When the cabbage has formed a suitably firm head then it is ready for harvesting – usually in about 65 days or so. Remove the mature cabbage by cutting at the base of the head, but leave the stem planted along with the outer leaves. The plant will then send up fresh shoots to form new heads.

Leave just 3 or 4 of these heads to develop and they will form miniature cabbages in just a few weeks. To store your cabbage head, make sure it is not wet to the touch, before wrapping in cling-film and storing in a cool place for no more than two weeks.

Carrots:

Introducing Carrots:

As it is for growing any vegetables, knowing how to grow carrots properly can save a lot of grief and heartache when it comes to harvest time. Carrots in particular are prone to a pest called the carrot fly (Chamaepsila rosae). This is a destructive pest also known to attack parsnips and celery, and so must be looked out for. That aside, growing carrots is not at all difficult if certain preparations are made that can ensure a good healthy crop of delicious fresh carrots for the table.

Just like onions, carrots are a chef's favourite as they can be included in a multitude of different dishes, and so are counted in the 'must have' vegetables in all the top restaurant kitchens. Being rich in vitamin A and calcium, carrots are delicious, steamed, boiled, and even roasted with a honey and orange glaze!

Ground conditions:
Carrots prefer a light sandy soil and preferably a situation where they can get most of the days sunshine; though they can stand a little shade, particularly in hotter climates. They must also be grown in soil that is free from stones, if you are to avoid the 'clubbing' effect that means the carrots grow all twisted and miss-shaped.

For this reason I always prefer to grow carrots in a raised bed, as it is easier to tend, and the soil can be better controlled to produce a sandy light soil, free from stones, that the growing carrots love.

Planting seed:
Once the soil or growing medium is prepared, then it is time to plant the carrot seed. This is a simple process that involves making a very shallow groove in the soil, and sprinkling the carrot seeds along the groove quite sparingly. Seed is then lightly covered up with soil. If planting before late march then they are best covered with a polythene cloche to encourage growth.

Rows should be approx. 6 inches apart. Shortly after the carrots have germinated, and have grown 2-3 inches in height; I would start to carefully thin out the plants to about 4 inches apart. To help avoid the dreaded carrot fly, be very careful with this process, causing as little disturbance as possible to the remaining plants. A handy tip would be to trim away the foliage of the seedlings you do not want, just below the surface.

For planting carrots in a straw bale please refer to the previous chapter 'Planting Tips & Techniques.'

Avoiding the carrot fly:
To begin with, after thinning remove all remaining foliage away from the carrot patch, as this will just attract the carrot fly.

Carrot fly is the carrots worst enemy by far. It is attracted to the smell of the carrot foliage, and from there descends to lay it's eggs at the base of the foliage where it meets the soil. It is the larva of the carrot fly that does the damage, by burrowing into the top of the carrot. First signs will be the leaves of the plant turning yellow, and the plant dying.

There is unfortunately no cure as yet for carrot fly devastation, but fortunately there are preventative measures you can take.

First of all is to keep in mind that carrot fly are low flying insects. For this reason it is best to grow the carrots in a raised bed if possible, about 18 inches (450mm) off the ground or more is preferred.

(It is worth noting here that as the straw bale itself is 18 inches high, carrot fly is not so much of a problem as it would be under normal growing conditions).

Next tip is to cover the plants with a fleece material to prevent the fly's from landing and laying their eggs on the carrots.

Try growing Allium plants such as garlic or chives, to help disguise the smell of the carrots and distract the fly from the growing carrots.

Harvesting/Storing:
From about July onwards, you now have a successful carrot crop to harvest – hopefully ! Mostly you just need to harvest the carrots as they are needed. However they can be stored by cutting off the foliage with sharp scissors about 1 inch above the carrot, then placing on a bed of dry sand, in a garden shed. Make sure the carrots do not touch, and inspect regularly to make sure there are none rotting.

This way the carrots can be kept fresh and wholesome over the winter months, but make sure they are kept frost-free and lightly covered over with sacking or some similar material. Knowing these basics of how to grow carrots should help ensure a healthy crop.

***

Cucumber:

Introducing Cucumbers:

A popular salad vegetable, this is a fast growing climbing plant that definitely prefers the heat; and if properly attended to, each plant will provide a number of fresh cucumbers throughout the growing season.

Planting:
The cucumber needs full sun and can be grown along the ground, or as a climbing plant growing up a trellis or garden net; therefore you must decide before planting just how you would prefer it to grow.

If planting from seed then grow inside in a warm place (65 degrees is needed for germination) and do not transplant outside until at least two weeks after the last frost.

Seeds should be sown in rows about 1 inch deep and 6 inches apart. Once they are ready for transplanting, then plant the young seedlings about 12-18 inches apart.

Cucumber is very susceptible to the frost so I would keep a fleece covering at hand to cover for the first week or so after planting.

Cucumbers prefer a neutral or slightly alkaline soil with a pH around 7. Compost with plenty of well-rotted manure and other organic material will produce an excellent crop.

Plant Care:
If your cucumbers are going to be lying on the ground, then lay them on a covering or straw to protect from the wet soil; this will also act as a mulch to prevent drying out. Hanging Cucumbers may have to be supported on the vine to prevent damage to the plant.

Cucumbers need constant watering as inconsistent watering can result in a small, bitter plant. However like most vegetables they will not tolerate over-watering. To avoid this, a quick tip is to stick your finger into the soil and if it is dry beyond the first joint then water is needed.

Harvesting:
Keeping your cucumbers harvested regularly will ensure a constant supply of fresh cucumbers. To maintain a healthy

crop you should harvest when they reach 6 inches and over; or if choosing to pickle them, around 2 inches is ideal.

Keep picking them as they grow on the vine as the vine will stop producing if they are not picked, and those that remain will become tough and slightly bitter.

As they are 90% water, cucumbers are better stored wrapped tightly in plastic film. They will last at least 7-10 days in this condition if stored in a cool place.

***

NOTES/ TO-DO PAGE

Green Beans:

Green Beans Introduction:

Growing runner beans (*Phaseolus coccineus*), is one of the most satisfying jobs around the vegetable garden for me. The reason I am enthusiastic about runner beans is that I am quite impatient by nature, and so can't wait for the crops to grow. This is where the runner beans come in handy – they grow so fast !

No sooner do you have the frame up, than they are reaching for the stars and in no time producing tasty beans. When planting runner beans, like any other plant really there are however a few steps to follow in order to get the best results.

Soil Conditions for Runner Beans:

Runner beans prefer a loamy soil mixed with a good compost mix, however they are a fairly forgiving plant and will grow in many soil types. Since beans take nitrogen from the air and deposit it in the soil, they need less fertilizer than most other plants and indeed are used in companion planting methods for this ability to deposit valuable nitrogen for other plants to benefit from.

Plant in full sun if possible, though some shade will be tolerated. They should be kept away from the wind, as they are likely to suffer from wind damage if too exposed.

Time for planting beans:

The time to plant your runner beans is after the last frost of the season, as runner beans are very susceptible to frost damage. Better to grow from seed in a cold-frame or greenhouse and then plant the young seedlings into the garden area. If there is a danger of a late frost, then it is better to cover at night with a light fleece to protect them.

Preparing for planting runner beans:

Before planting your runner beans, it is best to prepare the frame-work that will support them whilst growing. Mostly this is done with a wigwam type of frame, made up from several canes attached at the top and tied around with string.

The runner beans are then trained to grow up the canes, securing as they grow. This is slightly different from Peas which will secure themselves with tendrils from the plant. If planting seedling's then remove from the pot when they are well rooted, but not pot-bound in the container. Taking a small trowel, dig a hole big enough for the plug and place the plant in the hole, firming around the base with soil. Planting out under a cloche for the first few weeks of growing will also protect against the frost and give them a quick boost as the soil warms up.

This will also protect your young plants from the birds. Pigeon's in particular can do a lot of damage to a young bean crop, if it is not protected. Another way of protecting the early plants is to cut the bottom of a plastic coke bottle, and place over the plant (make sure you remove the top). Naturally this system is a bit more difficult if you already have your canes in place, so think ahead to exactly how you plan to proceed.

Rodents just love to nibble on a tasty bean ! Watch out for these and if it is a problem try covering with fleece to distract the mice during the early stages of growth. Many a bean crop has been destroyed by mice digging up the bean even before it has had a chance to sprout!

Planting your beans or peas within a cardboard toilet-roll holder is a great way to protect against cutworm and even mice! The cardboard will gradually rot away, but should last over the growing season.

Caring for your Runner Beans:
Generally speaking, runner beans need very little looking after, during the season. Water well when flowering starts in order to encourage growth. For the bushier type of bean

plants, nip out the growing tips as they reach the desired height.

Watch out for aphids, or caterpillars and take action at the first signs. Aphids can soon get out of control and be the cause of all kinds of plant disease, as well as contaminating your beans with a sticky mess!

Harvesting your Runner Beans:
All bean crops should be harvested when still young and small, for as they grow they can get quite tough and fibrous. Likewise they are best eaten immediately, or if headed for the freezer they should be blanched and frozen within the first few hours of picking to get the best flavor locked in.

Keep harvesting quite frequently, even if you do not need the beans. This encourages growth and ensures a steady supply of fresh succulent runner beans for the table. Beans can also be dried and stored for use in stews and casseroles, throughout the winter period.

Follow the same general advice for planting garden peas.

***

Leeks:

Introducing Leeks:

Leeks are probably one of the most sought after vegetables for the kitchen table, and knowing how to grow leeks essential for the vegetable gardener. producing a delicious long white bulb, as well as green leaves that can be used to flavour casseroles and soups, as well as countless other dishes; the leek is rich in vitamin A and so a great addition to the average diet.

The leek is of course the national symbol of Wales, as is the Thistle for Scotland, the Rose for England and the Shamrock for Ireland. As such, it is a well-known vegetable around the United Kingdom in particular.

Along with the decision to grow leeks, come's the decision on whether to grow from seedlings or indeed whether to grow your leeks direct from seed. This is along with the kind of leeks you wish to grow, and the ground conditions etc that are necessary for a good crop. These and other facts about growing leeks, will be explored in this article.

Ground conditions:
Leeks will grow in a wide mix of soil conditions, however to grow a good healthy crop of top leeks, there are certain rules you must follow - as is in fact the case with most plants of course.

First of all, it should be noted that the one ground condition that leeks do not thrive in, is boggy ground. So choosing good well drained ground in which to plant your seeds or seedling's is a first step to growing leeks.

Secondly, to produce the best crop, leeks should be grown in ground that has been heavily manured the previous year if possible. The reason for this is that if you plant leeks in freshly manured ground, then you will produce a very leafy crop which can be quite tough and stringy. Well-rotted compost is ideal to dig in before planting your leeks if organic matter is needed to enrich the soil.

Sowing Leeks - From seed:

If you are Sowing leeks from seed, then they should be sown very thinly about 1 inch (25mm) apart, in drills about 6 inches (150mm) apart. Plant just about 1/4 inch below the surface and lightly cover up. Sowing should be in the early spring around April time. If sowing direct into the seed bed, then placing a cloche over them for the first three weeks or so will encourage early growth as well as protecting from a spring frost.

After about two-three weeks, the leeks should have germinated. The next step is to thin out as soon as possible, so that the leek plants around two inches apart. When the plants are about 8 inches high in the early summer, then they are ready to plant in their permanent positions - if they are not already there. In any case they must now be thinned out to about 10 inches apart.

When re-planting your seedlings, use a dibber or a sharp stick to make a hole around 6 inches deep by two inches wide. Take your leek plant and trim the roots down to about one inch long (25mm) and clip just a little of the top of the leaves. After placing the leeks in the holes, top up with water. This will wash the soil around the base of the roots and enable the plant to get established quicker. Fill in the hole around the young plant.

How to grow leeks - in a trench:
Another way of growing leeks is the trench method, this is done by simply digging a trench in the planting area, about 1 foot deep (250mm) and placing about three inches of well-rotted manure at the bottom. The manure should be

covered by about 6 inches of soil. Carefully plant the leeks as described above and be sure that they are firmed around and perfectly upright. Plant about ten inches apart. If more than one trench is required, then dig them about two feet (600mm) apart in case the sides collapse during the work.

Caring for your leeks:
During the growing period, the leeks need minimal attention to be sure that the weeds are kept under control, by lightly hoeing between them. This helps to keep the soil loose which in turn helps with moisture retention. Another thing particular to leeks is Blanching.

This is a process designed to keep a nice length of white soft edible leek at the stem of the plant. Rather than letting it all go to leaf. One way to do this is to raise up the soil around the leek as it is growing, similar to the way that a potato harvest can have the drills raised around the young plants, to encourage growth of the tubers and also to stop the potatoes becoming exposed to the sun.

The problem with blanching your leeks is that they can become subject to rot, especially if the soil is particularly wet. This can however be prevented by fitting a collar to your leeks. This is simply a tube about 3 inches in diameter and up to 12 inches long. Push the collar into the soft earth around your leeks at or near the end of the growing season, usually around mid to late August, depending on the weather.

The collar can be made from almost anything, even brown paper tied on with elastic bands. The soil is then piled up against the plant as described. Taking these steps will help ensure that your leek harvest, which should be ready from late August right through to the late spring, is in peak condition and ready for the pot !

Leeks grown like this with a long white tuber, makes an absolutely tremendous 'leeks in cheese sauce' dish - one of my favourites.

Harvesting:
This should be done as and when you need them, leaving them in the ground until needed. Dig the leeks up with a garden fork, rather than just pulling from the ground, as this will result in you holding onto nothing but a handful of leaves! If you have to harvest them all, then store either in a box of sand in a cool place; or keep in a cool trench at the side of the plot if you need it for another harvest. Cover the roots lightly with soil, and pick when you need them.

Leek bulbs:
A handy by-product of leeks that have been left until the following summer, is leek bulbs. If the leek has gone to flower, then simply nip out the flower stems to get a nice harvest of leek bulbs at the stem of the plant in the summer. These can be used as onions or shallots for casseroles and stews etc.

***

Onions:

How to grow onions – Introduction:

To begin with, we must decide on whether to grow the onions from seed or from onion sets. The fact is that it is generally thought much easier to grow onions from sets rather than from the seeds themselves. It is also more likely that you will have a successful onion crop if you grow from the onion sets, unless you are a more experienced gardener and are well used to the intricacies of germinating and growing vegetables from seed.

How to grow onions - from sets:
As mentioned, it is generally thought of as a more guaranteed way to produce a good crop of onions, if you

grow from onion sets. There are a few basic things to go think about, before you simply plant your onion sets in the ground however. A few general rules of thumb to ensure your efforts are productive and the expenditure worthwhile, from both a financial and practical viewpoint.

Soil Condition:
Firstly, it is not considered wise to grow onions in the same bed for more than 3 years running, unless the previous crop has been disease free, and the soil is well fertilized and able to cope with the demands of the growing onions. As with most vegetable crops, it is better to rotate your plants around the growing area if this is possible, in order to 'spread the load' and give each plant the best possible chance of solid growth.

Onions should be planted as early as possible (around late Feb) to give as long a growing period as possible, in a soil ph of between 6 and 7.5 and should be planted in ground, that is well raked out to produce a fine tilth for planting the onions sets into. Preferably you will have turned over the ground and added some well-rotted manure the previous Autumn, this will ensure a good strong growth in the spring - if not; then remember it for next year :)

Planting:
After pressing down the area a little (onions prefer a firm bed), plant the onion sets about 4 inches apart, in rows set about 1 foot apart. This gives roof for the hoe when it comes to weeding between the rows. Plant the onions in a

small hole made with the trowel, and cover them up to the neck in soil.

Planting them like this will help prevent them climbing out of the ground as the roots start to take hold; with that in mind however, you will most likely have to re-set then a few weeks after planting to be sure this does not happen. A small sprinkling of grow-more will help at this stage to give the onion sets a quick boost.

When planting onion sets in a straw bale, you can use the method for seeds (cover the bale surface with soil), or press the onion set into individual prepared holes as described earlier. However I find that owing to the number of onions to a bale (16 or so), it is simpler and easier to use the seed method and simply press the onion sets into the soil.

Protecting from Birds:
Onions are not susceptible to birds like pigeons, in the same way that say for instance lettuce or cabbage is. However they are prone to inquisitive birds like Blackbirds and Crows, pigeons etc, that will pick them out of the ground and leave them lying on the surface. This is only usually a problem in the early stages of growth, and when the onion sets are properly rooted it is not so much of a problem. Nevertheless, if you are badly bothered with this happening to your onion sets then it is as well to put a fine mesh over them to protect the sets in the early stages of growth.

Harvesting:

Onions are ready to pick, usually around August, when the foliage becomes yellow and withers. Pick a dry day if possible and lift gently from the ground, leaving the onions to dry where they are for a day or two. They are then ready to store in a cool dry place, where they will last through-out the winter - provided you keep them free from frost damage.

Storing:
The dried withered Shaw's can be pleated together, enabling them to be hung up in bunches from the ceiling of your garden shed for instance. After about two weeks of drying out, the onions are ready to eat and should provide you with a fresh supply for the next few months - if you have grown enough!

Quick tip: Eat the ones with the thick necks first, as they do not last as well.

NOTES/ TO-DO PAGE

Potatoes:

How to grow potatoes - The basics:

Potatoes are perhaps the best vegetable to begin with if you are a new gardener, or if you have limited experience of growing vegetables, growing potatoes included. The reason is that potatoes grow in many types of soil conditions, and are fairly hardy against the weather, but do prefer cooler conditions. Once the potato shaws are through, they soon grow to block out any sunlight around their roots, which means that there is seldom any need to weed them, except in the most extreme of conditions - perhaps where the plot had not been properly weeded.

There can be few things more satisfying to a gardener, than digging up the potatoes at the end of the growing season. The reward for all your labours suddenly comes to the surface, it's a bit like a treasure hunt really - except that this is a treasure that you have planted, and are now getting it back with interest !

Buying Seed:

As well as knowing how to grow potatoes, you must know what kind of potatoes to grow. There are many different varieties of potatoes, some for baking, some for mashing. Potatoes that make the best fries etc etc. First rule though, especially to start with, is to find out just what varieties grow best in your area. The easy way to determine this is to go to a local supplier (not a large chain) as they will most probably stock the best varieties of potatoes for your specific region.

You must start with buying seed potatoes that are specifically reared for the purpose. You could just plant potatoes from the supermarket, however this is not such a good idea as they may have been sprayed with chemicals to prevent sprouting whilst in the shop for sale. You can in fact just plant potato peelings, if you are really stuck. As long as the potato peelings have an eye on them, they will grow - quite amazing really. I know I have in the past produced potatoes just from the peelings, though not the best crop - it is nevertheless possible, if you are on a very tight budget for instance.

Preparing Seed Potatoes:
The seed potatoes will often have begun to sprout, before you even get them out of the bag; this is a good thing. If not, then cover them over with a sack or generally keep them in a dark cool place for a few days, until they have sprouted even an inch or so. This is known as 'chitting' and means that they are ready for planting.

Preparing the ground:
Ground preparation for growing potatoes, is fairly straight forward. In fact potatoes are an excellent first crop where perhaps nothing has been cultivated before, as they are good for breaking up the ground. The soil just has to be dug over, preferably at the end of the previous growing season; and then raked out to pick up the worst of the stones and weeds.

When this is done, then simply string out a straight line, as a guide. Then run the corner of your Dutch hoe along the line to create a shallow groove. To this you can add a sprinkling of 'grow more' or general fertilizer, before placing the seed potatoes about 10 inches (250mm) apart along the groove.

Continue this procedure keeping the lines about 24-30 ins (600-750mm) apart, to allow for the next stage.

Planting:
Place the potatoes shoot side up in the groove. It is often said to break away some of the shoots and just leave one or two, personally I don't bother with that and just place them as they come. It doesn't seem to affect my potato harvest either way.
When this is done, then pick up the Dutch hoe again and lift the soil, first along one side, and then the other. This will form a mound along the length of the track, in which the potatoes will grow.

Some people I know, avoid this step and just place the potatoes in the ground without forming drills along the line of the crop. In my view this is the lazy man's way out, and is a mistake as it will lead to a crop that is more difficult to harvest, resulting in broken potatoes. It will also mean a poorer harvest in terms of the potatoes produced.

Back to creating the drills. After the first lift, then you wait until she shaws present themselves through the earth for a couple of inches. Go over the drills again with the Dutch hoe, and lift the soil to cover the new growth.

That's it, job done! As the potatoes grow then water them if need be, and look out for any predations of any kind. All being well then you can look forward to a harvest of great fresh grown potatoes in the Autumn.

For planting in Straw Bales. After the priming stage is complete simply sink the potato down into the bale until it's about 6 inches from the bottom, Being careful not to break away any shoots in the process.

Make sure at least one eye or shoot is pointing upward. Do not close up the channel above the potato entirely so that a little light gets through to the seed. This means that the plant will push up towards the light.

As the potatoes are grown from the stem of the plant rather than the roots, you will have potatoes all the way up to the top of the bale. This is in effect the same idea as growing potatoes in a barrel or tall container.

To harvest the potatoes simply cut away the string around the bale when the plant has died away at the end of the season. The bale can then be pulled apart to expose your potato harvest.

No more slicing the tubers with the garden fork!

Plant Care:
One word of caution is to look out for the signs of potato blight. This is a virus that can sometimes attach to and destroy your crop, and usually takes effect just before harvest time. The first sign of potato blight is a sudden

yellowing of the leaves, which soon begin to rot and fall over.

This is a disease that starts in the leaves and goes down into the tuber itself. Rather than try to prevent this happening, which is very difficult. I often harvest the entire crop before the disease has time to infect the potato. Ok, the potatoes may not have grown to their fullest potential, but at least I will have a partial crop of good healthy spuds.

An easy way to tell if it is to late, is to cut one of the tubers in half. You will see a dark vein throughout the tuber itself. If this is the case then simply dump them – not in the compost tip though, as the virus can remain in the soil for years.

If you try and store potatoes that have the potato blight in them, you will find that they will rot down to a smelly mush – really does spoil your day if you reach into a bag for your potatoes and you sink wrist deep into a rotting spud!!

Harvesting/Storage:
Potatoes can be harvested throughout their growing cycle, as soon as tubers begin to appear; this is particularly the case if you are happy with small 'new' potatoes renowned for their flavour. However to get the best out of your crop, wait until the leaves and shaws dry out at the end of the growing season, then lift with a garden fork – removing as much of the soil as possible before storing in a cool frost-free place.

The potatoes will last right over the winter if protected against the frost. This can be easily achieved in a barn or shed by covering with straw or sacking.

***

Tomatoes:

Introducing Tomatoes:

Growing Tomatoes, or any vegetable for that matter, can be a very rewarding and satisfying thing to do. Not only do you have the satisfaction of eating quality vegetables produced by your own hand, but you can also save a small fortune on the shopping bills as well – a real win, win situation.

As always when growing any vegetable, we must first of all decide just where we plan to grow them, For instance growing tomatoes outdoors in the deep south of the USA is just a little different from growing them in Scotland where they definitely need the benefit of a heated greenhouse!

Soil conditions as well as weather or temperature conditions, have always to be taken into account. Tomatoes thrive in full sun and in a temperature of between 70F / 21C and 89F / 29C, and thrive best in a well fertilized soil especially when the fruit is starting to grow on the stems.

Planting:
Although they can be grown from seed – which will give you a better choice of varieties – I find it preferable to buy the young plants at about 6-8 inches tall and transplant them into the prepared area.
They prefer well-drained compost with plenty of organic matter and well-rotted manure. Support will have to be provided in the form of canes, string, mesh or tomato cages. This is especially so in the beefsteak varieties (some weighing up to 1lb), that will produce a crop liable to put a heavy strain on the stem if not properly supported.

When feeding organic Tomatoes – which should be started when the first fruits start to appear - I always prefer a 'Tea' mixture of horse manure mixed with water, when it comes to 'feeding time', which would be about a ladle full once or twice a day when the tomatoes are in full growth. It goes without saying that care must be taken when handling any kind of manure or rotting material.

The cleaner way would be of course to just go for a more commercial tomato feed – there are loads on the market – however just as many precautions have to be taken when handling chemical feeds also, so I suppose it's a matter of choosing your 'poison'!

Organic growing methods are most certainly in the ascendancy though, and feeding methods I used as a boy to save money, are now all the rage – go figure.

Greenhouse Tomatoes:
Quite apart from the fact that tomatoes have to be grown in greenhouses in m any northern regions that are not warm enough for them; growing tomatoes in a greenhouse means that you can start a lot earlier in the season, just make sure that you have a small heat source going to keep away a late frost or the cool spring evenings.

Tomatoes can be grown in many types of containers, indoors and out. However be aware that they cannot stand frost at all, so be sure to protect them from it at all costs. As the season progress and the temperature heats up, then it is time to open the vents to try and maintain a constant temp around 80F or so. Care must be taken to water them regularly, and try and avoid splashing the leaves of the plant as this will result in the leaves being burned in the hot sun.

As the plants grow, and the tomatoes start to show, then I would normally trim away the excess leaves about halfway up the plant. This will concentrate the plant on producing tomatoes and not just filling the leaves. Side shoots should also be nipped away using your thumb and forefinger, as they will just take energy away from your tomatoes in the main stem.

Avoiding pests:

Pest control is an on-going labour for all gardeners, without doubt. Growing tomatoes in a greenhouse means that they are perhaps not quite so prone to the ravages of caterpillars, they can usually be fairly easily spotted and disposed of if they do appear. However Tomato plants are very susceptible to the ravages of Aphids such as greenfly and blackfly . To control Aphids with the use of chemicals is probably the most popular and perhaps the easiest.

It has to be said however that any chemicals that you use on your food plants, is likely to remain to some degree at least on the fruit or vegetables treated. The solution may be to go Organic and consider other alternatives to chemicals, such as a tablespoon of Canola oil and a few drops of Ivory soap into a quart of water. Shake the mixture well and pour into a spray bottle. Spraying from the top of the plant down, be sure to get the underside of the leaves for critters hiding there.

Support:

Just to emphasize the advice above - there is no definitive way of supporting your tomato plants as they grow, but they must be supported. Canes are the most popular, although string set into a spike in the ground at the tomato plant base and tied to a supporting beam in the greenhouse roof works just as well.

Make sure the plants are well tied to the string or cane – without choking the stem – and that the weight of the tomatoes does not pull them down.

Growing Outdoors:
Growing tomatoes outdoors is the privilege of those that live in warmer climates – unlike Scotland ! The principle however is pretty much the same.
The differences are mainly that the overall temperature cannot be maintained as well, and that outdoor tomatoes are more susceptible to the predations of pest's such as caterpillars, slugs etc. In fact the main difference is that they are more exposed and so vulnerable you could say.

Feeding the tomatoes is the same as indoors, although if you have a good fertile soil then it may not be so often. Insect control is of course on-going, and birds will have to be kept at bay by garden mesh. As for the predations of Rabbits, they do not seem so keen on tomato plants, but they will chew on them just for the hell of it – so best to keep them away by any means possible.

Harvesting:
Tomatoes are best eaten within days of plucking in order to get the best flavour possible; however if storing simply place in a paper bag and keep stem-up in a cool dark place. Contrary to popular belief green tomatoes do not ripen well on a window sill – they are more prone to rotting.

Best time to pick is when the tomato is firm and bright red (or yellow?) in color – depending on the variety of course. They can be kept in the fridge for a few days, but in doing so you will lose much of the natural tomato flavour.

***

From The Author:

Vegetable Gardening has certainly grabbed the imagination of the public in a way that I have never witness before. Whether this is because of the cost of food, or the environmental issues involved with growing vegetables commercially – or indeed whether it is potential 'Preppers' getting themselves prepared for Armageddon in one form or another; I really could not say.

More probable is that it is a combination of all three! Whatever the reason though, it is very welcome in my mind because at last folks are awakening to the benefits in physical and mental health, in environmental awareness and in financial benefits to be gained.

With the 'no-dig' vegetable gardening ideas such as Raised Bed gardening, Square Foot gardening, Container gardening and now Straw Bale gardening.

The ability to grow your own vegetables is open to just about anybody with the will to do so.

I sincerely hope that you have enjoyed reading the information contained within this book, and if you have not already done so – put the ideas into practice!

If you would like to leave a comment or review on Amazon I would be delighted to read it.

Meanwhile feel free to check out my other publications by clicking on the links below, or by visiting my Amazon authors page.

Thanks a million you for your purchase – it is much appreciated.

<u>Other Relevant Titles by James Paris</u>

<u>Raised Bed Gardening 5 Book Bundle</u>

<u>Companion Planting</u>

<u>Growing Berries</u>

<u>Square Foot Gardening</u>

<u>Compost 101</u>

<u>Vegetable Gardening Basics</u>

<u>Small Garden Ideas</u>

James Paris is an **Amazon Best Selling Author**, you can see the full range of books on his Amazon author page here..

<u>http://amazon.com/author/jamesparis</u>

NOTES/ TO-DO PAGE

NOTES/ TO-DO PAGE

Printed in Great Britain
by Amazon